GW00648943

Francis Frith's
Around Bradford

Photographic Memories

Francis Frith's
Around
Bradford

Revised and enlarged edition of original work by

Clive Hardy

First published in the United Kingdom in 1998
by WBC Ltd

Revised paperback edition published in the United Kingdom
in 2000 by Frith Book Company Ltd

Reprinted in paperback 2004
ISBN 1-85937-204-X

British Library Cataloguing in Publication Data

Francis Frith's Around Bradford
Based on an original work by Clive Hardy
ISBN 1-85937-204-x

Frith Book Company Ltd
Frith's Barn, Teffont,
Salisbury, Wiltshire SP3 5QP
Tel: +44 (0) 1722 716 376
Email: info@francisfrith.co.uk
www.francisfrith.co.uk

Printed and bound in Great Britain

Front Cover: The Mechanics' Institute 1897 39514

*The colour-tinting is for illustrative purposes only, and is not intended
to be historically accurate*

AS WITH ANY HISTORICAL DATABASE THE FRITH ARCHIVE
IS CONSTANTLY BEING CORRECTED AND IMPROVED AND THE
PUBLISHERS WOULD WELCOME INFORMATION ON OMISSIONS
OR INACCURACIES

Contents

Francis Frith: *Victorian Pioneer*

FRANCIS FRITH, Victorian founder of the world-famous photographic archive, was a complex and multi-talented man. A devout Quaker and a highly successful Victorian businessman, he was both philosophical by nature and pioneering in outlook.

By 1855 Francis Frith had already established a wholesale grocery business in Liverpool, and sold it for the astonishing sum of £200,000, which is the equivalent today of over £15,000,000. Now a very rich man, he was able to indulge his passion for travel. As a child he had pored over travel books written by early explorers, and his fancy and imagination had been stirred by family holidays to the sublime mountain regions of Wales and Scotland. 'What a lands of spirit-stirring and enriching scenes and places!' he had written. He was to return to these scenes of grandeur in later years to 'recapture the thousands of vivid and tender memories', but with a different purpose. Now in his thirties, and captivated by the new science of photography, Frith set out on a series of pioneering journeys to the Nile regions that occupied him from 1856 until 1860.

Intrigue and Adventure

He took with him on his travels a specially-designed wicker carriage that acted as both dark-room and sleeping chamber. These far-flung journeys were packed with intrigue and adventure. In his life story, written when he was sixty-three, Frith tells of being held captive by bandits, and of fighting 'an awful midnight battle to the very point of surrender with a deadly pack of hungry, wild dogs'. Sporting flowing Arab costume, Frith arrived at Akaba by camel sixty years before Lawrence, where he encountered 'desert princes and rival sheikhs, blazing with jewel-hilted swords'.

During these extraordinary adventures he was assiduously exploring the desert regions bordering the Nile and patiently recording the antiquities and peoples with his camera. He was the first photographer to venture beyond the sixth cataract. Africa was still the mysterious 'Dark Continent', and Stanley and Livingstone's historic meeting was a decade into the future. The conditions for picture taking confound belief. He laboured for hours in his wicker dark-room in the sweltering heat of the desert, while the volatile chemicals fizzed dangerously in their trays. Often he was forced to work in remote tombs and caves where conditions were cooler. Back in London he exhibited his photographs and was 'rapturously cheered' by members of the Royal Society. His reputation as a photographer was made overnight. An eminent modern historian has likened their impact on the population of the time to that on our own generation of the first photographs taken on the surface of the moon.

Venture of a Life-Time

Characteristically, Frith quickly spotted the opportunity to create a new business as a specialist publisher of photographs. He lived in an era of immense and sometimes violent change. For the poor in the early part of Victoria's reign work was a drudge and the hours long, and people had precious little free time to enjoy themselves. Most had no transport other than a cart or gig at their disposal, and had not travelled far beyond the

boundaries of their own town or village. However, by the 1870s, the railways had threaded their way across the country, and Bank Holidays and half-day Saturdays had been made obligatory by Act of Parliament. All of a sudden the ordinary working man and his family were able to enjoy days out and see a little more of the world.

With characteristic business acumen, Francis Frith foresaw that these new tourists would enjoy having souvenirs to commemorate their days out. In 1860 he married Mary Ann Rosling and set out with the intention of photographing every city, town and village in Britain. For the next thirty years he travelled the country by train and by pony and trap, producing fine photographs of seaside resorts and beauty spots that were keenly bought by millions of Victorians. These prints were painstakingly pasted into family albums and pored over during the dark nights of winter, rekindling precious memories of summer excursions.

The Rise of Frith & Co

Frith's studio was soon supplying retail shops all over the country. To meet the demand he gathered about him a small team of photographers, and published the work of independent artist-photographers of the calibre of Roger Fenton and Francis Bedford. In order to gain some understanding of the scale of Frith's business one only has to look at the catalogue issued by Frith & Co in 1886: it runs to some 670 pages, listing not only many thousands of views of the British Isles but also many photographs of most European countries, and China, Japan, the USA and

Canada – note the sample page shown above from the hand-written *Frith & Co* ledgers detailing pictures taken. By 1890 Frith had created the greatest specialist photographic publishing company in the world, with over 2,000 outlets – more than the combined number that Boots and W H Smith have today! The picture on the right shows the *Frith & Co* display board at Ingleton in the Yorkshire Dales (left of window). Beautifully constructed with a mahogany frame and gilt inserts, it could display up to a dozen local scenes.

Postcard Bonanza

The ever-popular holiday postcard we know today took many years to develop. In 1870 the Post Office issued the first plain cards, with a pre-printed stamp on one face. In 1894 they allowed other publishers' cards to be sent through the mail with an attached adhesive halfpenny stamp. Demand grew rapidly, and in 1895 a new size of postcard was permitted called the court card, but there was little room for illustration. In 1899, a year after Frith's death, a new card measuring 5.5 x 3.5 inches became the standard format, but it was not until 1902 that the divided back came into being, with address and message on one face and a full-size illustration on the other. *Frith & Co* were in the vanguard of postcard development, and Frith's sons Eustace and Cyril continued their father's monumental task, expanding the number of views offered to the public and recording more and more places in Britain, as the coasts and countryside were opened up to mass travel.

Francis Frith died in 1898 at his villa in Cannes, his great project still growing. The archive he created continued in business for another seventy years. By 1970 it contained over a third of a million pictures of 7,000 cities, towns and villages. The massive photographic record Frith has left to us stands as a living monument to a special and very remarkable man.

Frith's Archive: *A Unique Legacy*

FRANCIS FRITH'S legacy to us today is of immense significance and value, for the magnificent archive of evocative photographs he created provides a unique record of change in 7,000 cities, towns and villages throughout Britain over a century and more. Frith and his fellow studio photographers revisited locations many times down the years to update their views, compiling for us an enthralling and colourful pageant of British life and character.

We tend to think of Frith's sepia views of Britain as nostalgic, for most of us use them to conjure up memories of places in our own lives with which we have family associations. It often makes us forget that to Francis Frith they were records of daily life as it was actually being lived in the cities, towns and villages of his day. The Victorian age was one of great and often bewildering change for ordinary people, and though the pictures evoke an impression of slower times, life was as busy and hectic as it is today.

We are fortunate that Frith was a photographer of the people, dedicated to recording the minutiae of everyday life. For it is this sheer wealth of visual data, the painstaking chronicle of changes in dress, transport, street layouts, buildings, housing, engineering and landscape that captivates us so much today. His remarkable images offer us a powerful link with the past and with the lives of our ancestors.

Today's Technology

Computers have now made it possible for Frith's many thousands of images to be accessed almost instantly. In the Frith archive today, each photograph is carefully 'digitised' then stored on a CD Rom. Frith archivists can locate a single photograph amongst thousands within seconds. Views can be catalogued and sorted under a variety of categories of place and content to the immediate benefit of researchers.

Inexpensive reference prints can be created for them at the touch of a mouse button, and a wide range of books and other printed materials assembled and published for a wider, more general readership - in the next twelve months over a hundred Frith local history titles will be published! The day-to-day workings of the archive are very different from how they were in Francis Frith's time: imagine the herculean task of sorting through eleven tons of glass negatives as Frith had to do to locate a particular

See Frith at www.francisfrith.co.uk

sequence of pictures! Yet the archive still prides itself on maintaining the same high standards of excellence laid down by Francis Frith, including the painstaking cataloguing and indexing of every view.

It is curious to reflect on how the internet now allows researchers in America and elsewhere greater instant access to the archive than Frith himself ever enjoyed. Many thousands of individual views can be called up on screen within seconds on one of the Frith internet sites, enabling people living continents away to revisit the streets of their ancestral home town, or view places in Britain where they have enjoyed holidays. Many overseas researchers welcome the chance to view special theme selections, such as transport, sports, costume and ancient monuments.

We are certain that Francis Frith would have heartily approved of these modern developments in imaging techniques, for he himself was always working at the very limits of Victorian photographic technology.

The Value of the Archive Today

Because of the benefits brought by the computer, Frith's images are increasingly studied by social historians, by researchers into genealogy and ancestory, by architects, town planners, and by teachers and schoolchildren involved in local history projects.

In addition, the archive offers every one of us an opportunity to examine the places where we and our families have lived and worked down the years. Highly successful in Frith's own era, the archive is now, a century and more on, entering a new phase of popularity.

The Past in Tune with the Future

Historians consider the Francis Frith Collection to be of prime national importance. It is the only archive of its kind remaining in private ownership and has been valued at a million pounds. However, this figure is now rapidly increasing as digital technology enables more and more people around the world to enjoy its benefits.

Francis Frith's archive is now housed in an historic timber barn in the beautiful village of Teffont in Wiltshire. Its founder would not recognize the archive office as it is today. In place of the many thousands of dusty boxes containing glass plate negatives and an all-pervading odour of photographic chemicals, there are now ranks of computer screens. He would be amazed to watch his images travelling round the world at unimaginable speeds through network and internet lines.

The archive's future is both bright and exciting. Francis Frith, with his unshakeable belief in making photographs available to the greatest number of people, would undoubtedly approve of what is being done today with his lifetime's work. His photographs, depicting our shared past, are now bringing pleasure and enlightenment to millions around the world a century and more after his death.

Bradford - *An Introduction*

MANY OF the photographs appearing in this selection from the Frith Collection were taken in the 1880s and 90s. It was a time when Bradford was the centre of the woollen and worsted industry not only in this country, but throughout the world. However, the city's manufacturers were suffering from the effects of import tariffs imposed by a number of European countries - and there was worse to come. The McKinley Tariffs of 1895 resulted in the halving of British woollen and worsted exports to the USA. Even so, the late Victorian traveller would have found the city a veritable forest of smoking mill chimneys interspersed with the often squalid housing of

the workers. Streams and brooks ran black, polluted with mill waste and sewage. There were other industries, too. Bradford was on the western edge of the great Yorkshire coalfield; because the coal was near to the surface, it could be mined relatively inexpensively. Also close by were the ironworks of Bowling and Low Moor.

For centuries Bradford had grown slowly. The first written account we have comes from the Domesday Book. The entry covers the village itself together with several outlying hamlets and a number of manors. The total population was almost certainly less than one thousand, of which a couple of hundred or so would be living in Bradford. The biggest landowner in the area was a man named Gamel. Of Norse descent, Gamel farmed a number of plots throughout the area, which amounted to 1,500 acres.

BRADFORD AND THE WOOLLEN INDUSTRY

Just when Bradford's association with the woollen industry began is unknown. However, we do know that some weaving was being carried out in the area during the late 13th century, as an Inquisition from that era mentions the fining and imprisonment of one Evan of Gumersal, a weaver. In other parts of the county, cloth-making was fairly widespread, though on a small scale. The only exceptions to this were York and later Beverley, both of which had weaving guilds - York's was founded as early as 1150.

Without doubt, the major influence on Yorkshire's medieval development were the great Cistercian abbeys, such as Fountains, Rievaulx, Jervaulx and Kirkstall. Founded in poverty, the abbeys grew rich and powerful as a result of generous donations of land from Norman lords. It was on these lands that the abbeys reared sheep for their wool; at one time Fountains Abbey had 600,000 acres devoted to sheep pasture.

Most English wool was not woven at home but exported to Flanders and Lombardy. In order to finance some of their building programmes, monasteries would sell several years' wool production in advance by means of forward contracts. Sometimes this went wrong, leaving the monks well and truly in the red. In 1275 the Jews of York bailed out Fountains Abbey, which was over £6,000 in debt - a phenomenal amount of money in those days.

The abbey most closely associated with Bradford was Kirkstall. Founded under the patronage of Henry de Lacy, Lord of Pontefract, the monks of Kirkstall had first settled at Barnoldswick-in-Craven, but moved to the banks of the Aire in 1152. Kirkstall was given lands around Bradford and the charter to hold Wibsey Fair.

The 14th century saw a significant increase in the amount of cloth woven in England and in the export of manufactured cloth to the Continent. This was due to a number of factors, including the introduction of the spinning wheel into more rural areas, and a policy that actively encouraged Flemish weavers to come and settle in Yorkshire. For the most part the type of cloth produced was only one yard wide; anything wider required a broadloom, which had to be worked by two men.

Towards the latter part of the 17th century, the spinning of worsted yarn gained a foothold around Halifax and Bradford. Apparently there had been some production in Yorkshire as early as the 14th century, but by far and away the main centre for its manufacture was East Anglia. All this was about to change. Thanks to men like John Hustler of Bradford, Yorkshire would replace East Anglia as the country's principal manufacturer of worsted.

Hustler, born in 1714, became a master manufacturer and merchant, and later served on the Worsted Committee - a body set up by the manufacturers to regulate and police the industry in an attempt to combat mounting fraud and theft among suppliers and outworkers. The Worsted Acts of 1777 allowed for the establishment of an inspectorate whose job it was to investigate possible cases of fraud and, if necessary, bring the transgressors to court. Hustler had been involved with a combination of manufacturers between 1754 and 1776, and it was this experience that led to his being appointed chairman of the Yorkshire committee. The committee brought a measure of co-ordination to the industry that was to see trade continue to develop and put Yorkshire at the centre of the woollen and worsted industry. By 1773, such was the importance of worsted to Bradford that local manufacturers clubbed together to pay for a Piece Hall specialising in the sale of this type of cloth. In 1779 Halifax opened its rather grand 315-room Piece Hall,

but here dealers traded in both worsted and woollen cloths.

THE FACTORY AGE

The prospect of work in the new factories attracted thousands of people from rural areas to the textile towns of Lancashire and Yorkshire. Starting work in a factory in the early 19th century would have been unlike anything they had known before. There were strict hours of attendance, and work was carried out at a pace set by the employer in conditions that were virtually unregulated. People, including children,

Manningham Lane c1950 B173003

worked long hours - Bradford mill owners were among those who used orphans sent from London workhouses as little more than slave labour. Children as young as five worked up to 13 hours a day and were beaten to keep them awake.

Living conditions were often appalling. Families were crowded into single rooms or cellars and sanitation usually consisted of a cesspit, the contents of which invariably managed to contaminate the local water supply, normally a communal well. It took several outbreaks of cholera resulting in thousands of deaths to galvanise the country into public health measures.

Hand-weaving was considered a man's job. Power looms did not make much of an impression in Bradford mills until the 1830s, but once their advantages were seen they soon took over, enabling women and girls to weave. Mechanisation had long been viewed with suspicion by mill workers fearing for their jobs. This fear manifested itself in Luddism - the Luddites refused point blank to accept technical innovation.

The first serious problems occurred in 1811-12, when hand croppers rebelled against the introduction of shearing frames. Mills were attacked, frames destroyed and manufacturers threatened. Mill-owner William Horsfall was shot dead by Luddites on Crosland Moor. The Luddites were ruthlessly put down, with Horsfall's murderers paying with their lives on the gallows at York Castle. In the 1820s, violence erupted once more over the introduction of power looms and mechanical combing machines. In 1822 a power loom was smuggled into a mill at Shipley, but word soon got out and the place was surrounded by angry weavers. The loom was dismantled and taken away, but the cart on which it was being carried was attacked. The remains of the loom were dragged in triumph through the streets of Baildon.

There were attempts to improve working conditions in the mill towns. Men such as Richard Oastler and John Wood petitioned parliament to cut factory hours and end child labour in the mills. By the 1850s some workers were getting a few days' holiday, even if it was without pay, and there was at least some time off at weekends.

A world away from industrial unrest was the Great Exhibition of 1851, which proved a hit with Bradford mill workers. Travel agent Thomas Cook would send his son from Derby to Bradford on a Friday with several trains of empty carriages. John then toured the streets in a van accompanied by a band and persuaded the workers to part with five shillings each for their train fares. It is said that the local pawnshops were full of watches, deposited by workers raising extra cash for spending money.

TITUS SALT AND SAMUEL LISTER

Between them, Titus Salt and Samuel Lister were two of the most influential people in the history of Bradford. Titus Salt and his family moved to Bradford from Wakefield. Titus was apprenticed as a woolcomber, after which he landed a partnership with Daniel Salt & Son. The story of how Titus made his fortune is well known, but it was not his first venture. Titus acquired a large shipment of Russian Donskoi wool, but found it impossible to sell it on. Not to be outdone, he took over a mill and had the wool spun himself. The wool made an excellent yarn and sold without difficulty. Titus's love affair with alpaca began when he spotted some unwanted bales in the warehouse. Taking a sample, he asked his father's opinion. His father advised him to leave well alone. Like most sons, Titus ignored his father's advice, bought the entire shipment and had it woven. Alpaca soon caught on, and the Salts prospered.

What set Titus apart from many other Bradford mill owners was his concern for the welfare of his workforce. Titus realised that a contented workforce meant better productivity, and better productivity meant that he would continue to prosper. It culminated in the building of a new mill and a village to house its workforce at Saltaire between 1850 and 1853. Titus provided his workers with a standard of accommodation far higher than most of them would ever have had in Bradford. He also built a school, almshouses and a cottage hospital, but no pubs as he was against alcohol.

Another well-known businessman was Samuel Cunliffe Lister, who came from a mill and quarry-owning family. Samuel gave up the manufacturing side of the business for a while to concentrate on woolcombing and the development of machinery for the worsted trade. He went into partnership with George Donnisthorpe, a mechanic from Leeds, who had developed a woolcombing machine. Samuel knew that George's design could be improved on, and in 1843 they produced their first samples of fine-combed Botany wool. They bought up most of the patents for combing machines, and put theirs on the market. With profits of £1,000 per machine, Lister became a very wealthy man, able to finance the building of his magnificent Manningham Mill. An enormous worsted and silk mill, Manningham had a total floor space of 26 acres. Its chimney, styled as an Italian campanile, is 255 ft high and is known as Lister's pride.

Between 1888 and 1893, the number of trade unionists almost doubled. In 1891 Bradford experienced a strike lasting five months; the reason was an imposed reduction in wages at Lister's mill due to a fall-off in orders. A meeting at St George's Hall ended with strikers clashing with police. The following night it is said that 20,000 people rioted, and troops were called in to assist the civil powers. On the third night a searchlight was mounted on the tower of the town hall and troops were again called in. There were a number of baton charges and arrests before the mob was finally dispersed. The strikers returned to work having gained nothing. A direct result of the Lister's strike was the founding of the Independent Labour Party at a conference held in the town in 1893. Among those present were Keir Hardie, George Bernard Shaw and Fred Jowett.

BY ROAD, RAIL AND CANAL

The 127-mile long Leeds & Liverpool canal was one of the great civil engineering projects of the 18th century. Authorised in 1770, the canal would, when completed, allow the passage of goods from the Mersey to the Humber. In 1778 three sections were open for traffic, but owing to problems with financing, construction came to a halt until a new money-raising Act was placed before Parliament in 1790. Work slowed down again in 1792 following the outbreak of war with France, and the canal was not completed until 1816. In spite of Bradford's growing importance, the nearest the canal got to the town was at

Shipley. It was not until 1820 that a three mile-long canal from Shipley to the centre of Bradford was opened.

There was a considerable amount of traffic between Bradford and Leeds, much of which was for onward shipment. Though the canal carried its fair share, the old Leeds-Bradford turnpike was extremely busy by the standards of the day; by 1830 it was becoming increasingly difficult to maintain. In that year there was a proposal to link the two towns by rail with a line running through Laisterdyke, Stanningley and Wortley. The scheme was abandoned owing to ever-increasing civil engineering estimates and hostility from landowners.

Bradford would not be served by a direct rail link until July 1846, when the Leeds & Bradford railway opened for traffic. Four years later, the Lancashire & Yorkshire railway reached the town, followed in 1854 by the Great Northern railway. Bradford was never to be on a through route, though the Midland railway had planned to build a new line from Royston via the Spen Valley to link up with the Shipley-Bradford line. Some work was done, but the project was finally killed off with the outbreak of the Great War.

Horton Park Bridge1897 39531

The City Centre and its Buildings

Left: **Darley Street 1897** 39508
This bustling cobbled street runs alongside the covered markets, which opened in the 1870s. Halfway up the street is a striking sign advertising a spectacle maker. These larger-than-life trade signs were essential in Georgian and Victorian times - many ordinary customers were unable to read. Further on up the street is public library, where a news room stayed open for the working man until 8pm. The street and its buildings cover what was once gardens and orchards.

Below: **Bank Street c1950** B173019
This view looks up towards Kirkgate and Darley Street from the Hustler Gate crossing. On the right is the Bradford branch of the National Provincial Bank.

Above: **Kirkgate,
Market Buildings
1897** 39507
In 1866 the Council
obtained market rights
from the Rawson family
at an annual rent of
£5,000 and built the
imposing Kirkgate
Market. With its public
abattoirs and wholesale
and retail area, it was
among the largest in the
country. The cost of
building it approached
£200,000.

Left: **Market Street
1897** 39509
A policeman stands in
the centre of the cobbled
intersection. A hundred
years earlier, Bradford's
6,000 inhabitants were
looked after by just two
constables and a handful
of deputies. There were
also six night watchmen
available, but they only
patrolled property
belonging to those
willing to pay for the
service. Further along is
another of Bradford's
fine civic buildings - the
Venetian Gothic-style
Exchange.

The Wool Exchange 1897 39512
Bradford's Wool Exchange, with its lofty facades, pointed arches and 150ft tower, was created in the grand Venetian Gothic style, and symbolised the wealth and prestige the textile industry had brought to the town. On 'change' days the atmosphere could be truly international, with buyers and sellers from around the world. It was said that no matter the type of wool or hair, a buyer would be found at the Bradford Exchange. The Wool Exchange was built to the design of the Bradford architects Lockwood and Mawson in 1867 - they were the winners of a competition for the most successful design. Lord Palmerston laid the foundation stone. It is said that when traders were about their buying and selling on Mondays and Thursdays, the place had the atmosphere of a madhouse.

The Mechanics' Institute 1897 39514
This view shows the Mechanics' Institute, at the corner of Market Street, which was built by Andrews and Pepper in 1871. In common with many of Bradford's Victorian public buildings, it is in the Italianate style, unfussy and restrained. On the corner are the premises of Matthews and Brooke, fine art dealers and picture frame makers.

The Technical College 1890 23495
In 1882 the college became independent from the Mechanics' Institute and was given its own premises. The town saw its college as essential to its efforts to keep abreast of competition from France in the production of quality woollen cloths.

Above: **Tyrrel Street 1897** 39510
This photograph shows Tyrrel Street at the intersection with Bridge Street. At the right-hand corner is the imposing Victorian shopfront of Butterfield's, the cutlers and opticians.

Left: **Tyrrel Street 1903** 49713
This classic and beautiful photograph shows this bustling shopping thoroughfare that runs adjacent to Market Street. On the left is Booth & Walker, one of Bradford's leading retail stores, famed for its china and glassware showrooms, and a little beyond the Orient Cafe, purveyors of Collinson's teas and coffees. There is standing-room only on the tram. The driver and conductor are chatting to the inspector. The system was electrified in 1897.

◀ **The Town Hall 1897** 39511
In April 1891, following two nights of trouble caused by strikers from Lister's factory, a searchlight was mounted on the tower of the Town Hall, and troops were brought in to assist the civil powers. A number of baton charges and arrests were made before the strikers were finally broken.

The Town Hall and Square 1903
49712

The splendid and distinctive Gothic Town Hall with its 200ft tower, modelled on the Palazzo Vecchio in Florence, was completed in 1873 at a cost of £100,000. It was designed by the Bradford architects Lockwood and Mawson to rival the new town halls of neighbouring Leeds and Halifax. By the time this photograph was taken, it was clearly showing the effects of thirty years exposure to industrial pollution. The building was given a thorough cleaning in the early 1970s. The campanile clock chimed the hours. The Town Hall was built on land which was once in the township of Horton.

▲ **The Town Hall 1888** 21007

The Council Chamber 1888
009

adford's Council Chamber is uated behind the Town Hall. is view shows the ornate s-lit interior. The designers, ckwood and Mawson, had eady earned wide acclaim r Salt's Mill, Saltaire and the ool Exchange. In 1895, adford Corporation was mposed of 45 councillors d 15 aldermen. The rough was divided into 15 rds.

▼ Towards Town Hall Square c1950 B173028

This photograph shows the approach to the Square just a few months before the abandonment of the tramway system in 1950 - at centre is a tram stop sign. In the background a trolleybus is about to pass a tram as it heads towards the Town Hall. View No. B173042 shows that a roundabout has been built over the old tramlines.

▼ Towards Town Hall Square c1955 B173042

On the right is the War Memorial, and in the distance the tower of the Town Hall. Out of sight on the left is the Alhambra.

▲ Town Hall Square c1950 B173030

The building rounding the corner on the left has been taken over by Burton the tailor. Later the Bradford branch of this nationally-known outfitter was to move to Darley Street. Two white-cuffed policemen are directing the traffic. A trolleybus is emerging from Tyrrel Street.

◄ **Town Hall Square c1950**
B173031
This view looks towards the Town Hall, which is out of sight on the right. Collinson's Cafe, in Tyrrel Street, has been given a facelift - it now occupies fashionable new premises, as white as sugar, sandwiched between two earlier, smoke-engrimed buildings. This busy junction is now a mess of building styles and untidy signs.

Forster Square 1897
39506
Forster Square lies at the very heart of the old town. On the right is the 1869 statue of Richard Oastler, who was the leading advocate for the ending of child labour in the mills. Children often worked thirteen hours a day in Bradford's factories, and were subjected to beatings to keep them awake. Poking into the view behind the statue is a steam tram engine. These noisy contraptions belched smoke; they were intended as an interim measure between horse-trams and an efficient electric street tramway system.

Forster Square 1903

49711

The previous photograph, taken five years earlier, shows cobbles lapping up to the foot of the statue to Forster, 'the Education King', erected in 1890. In 1882 the Broadstones area was cleared to make way for Forster Square. Part of the re-development included a post office; though impressive in its own right, it somewhat obscures the elevations of the parish church behind. On the extreme right are the stolid and monumental warehouses of the Bradford Dyers' Association, built in the mid 1860s. The area around is known as 'Little Germany', owing to the large numbers of Germans who colonised Bradford in the Victorian era and established warehouses.

The Post Office, Forster Square c1950 B173029
Bradford had an impressive postal network. This head office opened from seven in the morning to ten at night.
The branch in Tyrrel Street was connected to the head post office, shown above, by pneumatic tubes. There were
34 town sub-offices and 21 country sub-offices, at almost all of which customers could arrange money orders, use
the savings bank and send telegraphs. The Post Office, built in 1886, is now divided into offices.

Forster Square c1950 B173001
This broad open space was named in honour of William Edward Forster (1818-1886), the Member of Parliament
for Bradford and the minister responsible for the 1870 Education Act, which established compulsory state
elementary education. His statue is on the right.

Forster Square c1950 B173027
Note the web of trolley bus cabling strung out across the Square. In the background is the broad frontage of
Forster Square station, and on the right, by the triple-ridged iron roofs, the parcel depot. To the extreme right is
the YMCA.

Forster Square c1965 B173068
This photograph is a clear example of how town planning and development in the 1960s could be highly injurious
to our town centres. Here Victorian grandeur has given way to brash 20th-century functionalism. This colossal
glass structure makes no concessions whatsoever to local materials, existing rooflines or the scale of surrounding
buildings. Chain stores huddle in the shadows at its foot.

◀ **St Peter's Church, The Nave, Looking East 1890** 23499
The interior of the church was re-arranged in 1705, and galleries were added towards the close of the 18th century. The nave columns are slim and elegant, and the chancel arch broad and unfussy. Light floods in through the fine Victorian east window. During the Civil War, Francis Corker, the Vicar of St Peter's and a devout Royalist, helped to save Pontefract Castle from being taken by Parliament.

The Great Northern Victoria Hotel 1897 39521

The Great Northern Railway opened its terminus at Adolphus Street in 1854. However, from 1867 it shared a joint station (Bradford Exchange) with the Lancashire & Yorkshire. At this time the Victoria Hotel was built to cater for the new influx of rail travellers to the town. Though it is broadly Italianate in style, its twin roof domes suggest a French chateau. Rooms at the prestigious Victoria cost from 4s a night.

St Peter's Church (The Cathedral) 1923
74406

In December 1642, the Earl of Newcastle was approaching Bradford with a Royalist force. The town had declared for Parliament, and the parish church was being fortified. The tower was protected from cannon shot with sheets of wool, and it was here that the citizens made their stand.

St Peter's Church 1891 28297

St Peter's perches on a hillside above Forster Square, its sturdy tower peeping above the roofs. The church was built in the Perpendicular style in millstone grit; the nave and chancel were erected in 1458, and the tower half a century later. Though cathedral status had been granted to St Peter's in 1919, work on upgrading and extending the building did not begin until the 1950s. Among the improvements were a new chancel, a song room, and a vestry for the bishop.

▼ **The Children's Hospital 1897** 39523

Throughout much of the 19th century, Bradford's death rate among children under five years of age was a disgrace. In 1876 alone, over 2,000 of Bradford's under-fives died. This imposing building, its sparse decoration bringing it a somewhat severe appearance, was one of several charitable concerns in the town; they were founded in the later years of the century, when there was a more enlightened attitude to public health and welfare. As well as an Infirmary, there was an Eye and Ear Hospital, a Blind Institution, a Fever Hospital, and orphanages for both girls and boys (the boys' institution was the Nutter Orphanage).

▼ **The Infirmary 1897** 39522

Bradford was a pioneering town in matters of public health; it established one of the very earliest municipal hospitals in Britain, as well as separate medical and dental services for schools. During ward rounds, patients at the town infirmary had to stay still and lie at attention in their beds, and were instructed not to speak to the doctor or the matron unless they were asked a specific question.

▲ **St George's Hall 1897**
39517
This impressive structure was built in 1853 and resembles a classical temple, with a row of columns rising from the first floor. Until the Town Hall was completed, St George's was used for any council business where large numbers of people were expected to turn up: almost 4,000 could be seated. Charles Dickens and John Ruskin were just two of the many Victorian celebrities to speak here.

◄ **The Alhambra and the New Victoria c1950** B173009
The golden-domed Alhambra variety theatre was built in 1914, the vision of the impresario and 'King of Pantomime' Francis Laidler, and could seat 1,800. It was on a site near where the Alhambra stands that Bradford's first spinning mill was completed in 1800. In 1804 it was almost destroyed by fire. The New Victoria, constructed with two million bricks, echoes the Alhambra with its domes, and opened in 1930 as a cinema.

Left: **The Alhambra c1955** B173043
The town trolleybus was developed on the
Continent. Like the electric tramcar, it drew
current from an overhead power supply,
but did not require rails to run on. On 20
June 1911, a joint scheme between Leeds
and Bradford saw the inauguration of the
first trolleybus service in Great Britain. A
policeman, with long white cuffs, directs the
traffic past the Alhambra, with its splendid
dome.

Below: **The War Memorial 1923** 74404
Behind the memorial, with its powerful and
moving statues of soldiers, stands the
figure of Queen Victoria, sculpted by Alfred
Drury, and unveiled by HRH The Prince of
Wales in 1904 during his visit to the
Bradford Exhibition. On the right is the
façade of the Alhambra variety theatre.

**Manningham Lane
1902** 48570
This important
thoroughfare heads
westwards out of the
town. The building on
the left, with its
wrought-iron
colonnaded front, is the
Theatre Royal.
Workmen are up on
ladders repainting the
windows. It was here on
13 October 1905 that
Sir Henry Irving gave
his final performance.
After retiring to his
hotel for the night, he
was taken ill and died.
The Theatre Royal was
later used as a cinema,
and was eventually
demolished in 1976. In
the distance is the old
Yorkshire Penny Bank,
built in 1895.

Manningham Lane 1921 71623
This view looks towards the city centre, with Cheapside to the left and Darley Street to the right. The ornate white building on the right is the Regent Cinema and, out of sight on the left, is the Theatre Royal. Seventy years earlier, Thomas Cook's son had wandered the streets of Bradford, enticing workers to part with the five-shilling train fare for a trip to London to see the Great Exhibition in Hyde Park. It is said that the local pawnshops were full of watches left by workers raising the fare.

Manningham Lane c1950 B173020

The trams have been replaced by trolleybuses. Although Bradford was a pioneer of trolleybus operation, the first-ever conversion of an existing route from trams to trolleys was in Birmingham in 1922. Cinema goers to the Regent, out of sight on the left, were queuing that week to watch Clark Gable and Spencer Tracy in 'Boom Town'.

Bradford's Parks

Left: Lister Park, Boating on the Lake 1921
71629
The park boasted three acres of ornamental water, landscaped into sinuous curves. In the distance rowers are rounding a wooded island. In 1926 the boating was leased to Mr Fred Falkingham, who maintained a trim fleet of rowing-boats for visitors, as well a motor-launch. Manoeuvring the dinghy in such a tight space must have been a little daunting.

Above: **Lister Park, The Gateway 1897** 39524
This imposing gateway is not as ancient as it appears. It was created in the Norman style - with battlemented roofs, towers and portcullis - using stonework which had previously formed part of the structure of the old Christ Church, which stood In Darley Street.

Lister Park 1921 71624

This photo shows the broad entrance to Lister Park. The land at Manningham was purchased by the Corporation for £40,000 in 1870 - a fraction of its true worth. It was originally the ancestral home and estate of Samuel Cunliffe Lister, who was afterwards created Baron Masham. It consisted of a mansion and grounds, together with a deer park on the farther side of Jumbles Lane. A lodge was built here for the Park Ranger.

The Cartwright Memorial Museum 1921 71626

Samuel Cunliffe Lister's old mansion was demolished by the Corporation, and following a substantial donation of £47,000 from him, the Libraries and Art Gallery Committee erected the Cartwright Memorial Hall on the site in 1904.

The Cartwright Memorial Museum c1950 B173017
The Cartwright Memorial Museum was designed to house Bradford's art treasures, and was named in memory of
Dr Edmund Cartwright, who had invented the power loom. It was designed by J W Simpson and Allen in a
flamboyant Baroque style with a central turret and cupola.

Lister Park, The Lake c1950 B173021
In May 1904, Bradford turned out to welcome the Prince and Princess of Wales when they came to Lister Park to
open the Bradford Exhibition, an inaugural display of art treasures and industrial machinery. The lake was the
venue for naval battles using scaled-down models of warships. The exhibition was held throughout a memorably
hot summer and thousands of people thronged to enjoy the spectacle.

Lister Park, The Bandstand 1923
74400
To the rear of Cartwright Hall is this fine ornamental stone bandstand, built at a cost of over £600. A guidebook of the 1920s, by Joseph Bentley, reports that 'here on Sundays, Wednesdays and Saturdays, first-class military and other bands dispense music of the highest order, classical and popular, to the delight of thousands of sitters and promenaders'.

▼ **Lister Park, The Lake 1897** 39527
Townspeople visiting Lister Park could enjoy the exotic delights of the
Botanical Garden, swim in an open-air pool, play bowls, and enjoy
games of tennis and putting.

▼ **Peel Park 1897** 39530
In 1874 the park was the venue for celebrations, including a spectacular
fireworks display, to mark the unveiling of a statue to Sir Titus Salt. When
the park was first mooted, Sir Titus gave £1,000 towards the cost. Note
the ornamental fountain and Chinese-style lattice bridge.

▲ **Peel Park 1897** 39529
Bradford's first public
park was Peel Park,
opened in 1863 and
named in honour of Sir
Robert Peel, who had
been instrumental in the
abolition of the Corn
Laws. At Whitsun the
park was packed with
people enjoying the
entertainments of the
Great West Riding Galas,
which were promoted by
the Bradford Hospital and
Convalescent Fund.

◄ **Peel Park 1897** 39528
This peaceful scene in Peel Park shows how municipal-style, regimental planting was a natural product of the 19th century, reflecting the Victorian desire for social control. The city parks were playgrounds for the working man, and the city fathers considered it important that he be presented with a model symbolizing organised society.

Around Bradford

Above: **Saltaire, General View 1893** 33186
Saltaire is set on the River Aire at the northern edge of Shipley, fringed by the broad expanse of Baildon Moor. In this photograph the chimneys of Titus Salt's six-storey textile mill, designed by the celebrated engineer Sir William Fairburn, soar over the landscape.

Left: **Saltaire, The Railway Station 1909** 61871
Saltaire owes its existence to Sir Titus Salt, who moved his alpaca and mohair mills here in the 1850s. The railway station is on the Midland line from Bradford to Skipton. The railway station was opened in 1856. Titus Salt's Mill, some six storeys high, sits alongside the line. There was a siding close by with turntables, making it possible for raw wool to be carried right into the mill buildings. Titus Salt created a community very much to his own pattern at Saltaire. He refused to allow the construction of public houses here; the town remained 'dry' until recent times, because of Salt's firm belief in abstinence from alcohol. Though Titus was concerned for the welfare of his employees, he expected them to put in a fair day's work for their pay. As well as building Saltaire, Titus Salt donated well over £100,000 to various causes around Bradford. Salt's rules for workers living here were strict. Washing was not allowed to be hung out to dry (wash-houses were provided with wringing machines and drying closets).

◄ **Saltaire, Victoria Road 1893**
33188
Sir Titus was determined that his workers should have a healthier environment to live and work in. The workers' cottages he had built were made of stone lined with brick, and comprised a parlour, kitchen, and pantry, and from two to four bedrooms. When the village was completed there were 850 houses and 45 almshouses, as well as a range of civic buildings. The community was also pioneering in that the supervisors' houses were integrated amongst those of the ordinary mill workers.

◀ Saltaire, Salts Mill 1903 49705

Salts Mill was the largest in Europe: the weaving shed housed 1,200 looms and a workforce in excess of 3,000. The first mill building was erected in 1853, and a second in 1865. Increased competition from factories abroad finally forced its closure in 1986. Since then it has been given a new lease of life - it now incorporates several shops, three art galleries and industrial units for high-tech businesses.

▼ Saltaire, Salt School 1903

49704

Saltaire's school was built in 1877. One of its most famous pupils was Joseph Wright, who from the age of seven worked at Salts Mill. When he was older, he enrolled at the Bradford Mechanics' Institute and later at the Yorkshire College. He was admitted to Heidelberg University and gained a doctorate, later going on to become Professor of Comparative Philology at Oxford.

◀ Saltaire, The Institute 1893 33192

The Institute, built in 1871 at a cost of £25,000, contained a library, reading rooms, gymnasium, billiards room and lecture hall for 800 people. Titus Salt decreed that it should 'supply the advantages of a public house, without its evils'. There were two lions outside and two more across the road outside the school. They were originally to have graced Nelson's Column, but were considered too small.

Saltaire, Victoria Road 1909 61869
Saltaire's streets were named after members of Titus Salt's family. Salts Hospital opened in 1868, and treated in the main victims of accidents at the mill. There were only six beds. Inevitably, it grew into a hospital that looked after the health of the entire community. A third floor was added in 1909, together with four almshouses.

Saltaire, Roberts Park 1909 61872
Saltaire's park covers 14 acres; it was opened to the mill workers in 1871. Titus Salt stands in solitary dignity on his podium surveying the model village and green paradise he created. The park was planted with exotics and specimen shrubs and trees; it conjured up a very different world from that associated with the grime of factory life. At weekends, Salt's employees gathered in their hundreds around the bandstand to enjoy concerts. However, no spitting, stone throwing, gambling, begging or drinking were permitted.

Saltaire, The River Aire 1893 33191
The graceful River Aire winds down from Malham in the Dales by way of Skipton and Keighley. By the time it reaches Saltaire it is broad and sinuous, with broad banks studded with trees. By the 1860s the Aire was already suffering from the effects of pollution caused by outflow from Bradford's mills. In 1868 the corporation was successfully sued for failing to take steps to control waste disposal. The outcome of the case was the opening of Esholt Sewage Works.

Queensbury, Black Dyke Mills c1960 Q15007
Queensbury lies to the south-west of Bradford at 1,100 ft above sea level. The town was originally called Queen's Head, but the name was changed during the 19th century. It is the home of Foster's Black Dyke Mill, which opened in 1835. This photograph shows the entrance. Like Titus Salt, Foster saw the benefits to be had from promoting alpaca; both men enjoyed a virtual monopoly with this type of cloth until others followed their lead.

Queensbury, The Memorial c1960 Q15010
In the High Street, on the corner of Brighouse Road, is the Victoria Hall, comprising concert hall, lecture rooms and baths, which was built in 1888. In front of it is the imposing Albert Memorial, conceived by E Milnes of Bradford, and erected in 1863. It is in the form of an Eleanor cross, forty feet high, incorporating drinking fountains and a statue of the Consort within the arches.

Queensbury, Holy Trinity Church c1960 Q15016
This substantial church was built in 1849 and restored in 1885. It is in the Pointed style, and consists of nave, aisles and chancel, with a pinnacled tower and six bells. In the 1890s the value of the living was £340.

Queensbury, High Street c1960 Q15008 Queensbury is just over three miles south-west of Halifax. As well as being a centre for the textile industry, stone was quarried locally and coal worked. In the 1890s there was a popular summer fair, held in the week of the second Monday in August. Here we see the local branch of the National Provincial Bank, tucked in beside Rushworth's the newsagent. The latter has brickwork severely pointed in white.

◄ **Queensbury, The Old Raggalds Inn c1960** Q15013
This ancient inn on the Denholme to Queensbury road is said to have been built in the 1400s. Three years ago it underwent a major restoration, and was extended and considerably altered. It has been renamed the Raggalds Country Inn. The open moorland still stretches out behind the buildings, and sheep and cows graze the rough pastures. Websters Brewery has long since disappeared, and the inn is now a free house.

◀ **Eldwick, Dick Hudson's Pub 1921** 71288
On the edge of Eldwick Moor stands Dick Hudson's pub, once known more familiarly as the Fleece Inn. In the 19th century, the pub's celebrated landlord, Dick Hudson, was renowned for his delicious pies. Tourists visiting the moors would congregate here after a day's invigorating tramping to eat their fill.

▼ **Baildon, The View from the Bank c1960** B332020
Baildon is situated on a hilltop a mile and a half north of Shipley, close to Baildon Moor. It was through the streets of this old industrial town in 1822 that rioters dragged the remains of a power loom after the cart on which it was being carried was attacked. The parish church of St John the Evangelist, perched on Church Hill, in the distance, commands views of magnificent scenery. It was built in 1848. An electric tramway was constructed to aid access to the higher reaches of the Moor, where there are entrenchments and tumuli. The summer service was frequent owing to the great popularity of the area.

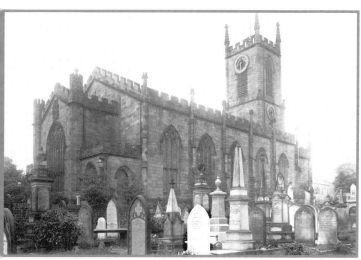

◀ **Shipley, St Paul's Church 1893** 33195
The expansive church, with its embattled tower, was erected in the Gothic style in 1825, and thoroughly restored and reseated in 1876, enabling almost 1,500 worshippers to attend services. It was at St Paul's that the funeral of Handel Parker took place in 1928. He worked as a woolcomber, but left when he was twenty to become a full-time musician. One of his most famous tunes is 'Deep Harmony', which the Black Dyke Mills band always played at the end of their concerts.

Shipley, The Park 1903 49701
Crowghyll Park was opened in 1890 on ground that had been formerly used as a quarry. Neat gravel paths fringed by well-tended flower and shrub beds lead to steps that climb up to St Paul's Church, which rises over the tree canopies behind.

Shipley, The Arndale Shopping Centre c1965 S122009
The shopping centre contrasts strongly with the older retail outlets and civic buildings of the town. The 1960s and 70s were bleak decades for town development. Planners clearly took little heed of existing buildings and local materials.

Shipley, Kirkgate c1965 S122014
Shipley was a centre for weaving and the scene of a near riot in 1822 when James Warbrick erected a power loom in a mill. The loom had been smuggled in, but word soon got out and the mill was surrounded by a mob of weavers. The loom was dismantled, but the cart carrying it away was attacked and the loom destroyed. It was at Shipley that the three-mile-long Bradford canal joined the Leeds & Liverpool canal. In Kirkgate, close by the church, is an old house of the 1590s, with mullioned windows and hoodmoulds.

Shipley, The Roundabout c1965 S122012

In the background are the former tram sheds, converted to house Shipley's complement of trolleybuses. Bradford was not only the first to introduce trolleybuses, but the last to discontinue their service - the system survived until 1972 when it was finally closed. There is a trio of collectable cars in the foreground - a Morris Minor and Countryman, and a Triumph Herald.

Shipley, The Manor House 1903 49699

This plain, ashlar house has a date of 1673 carved over the porch. In the 11th century, there were over 150 manors in the area between the Aire and Calder, Pontefract and Clitheroe. They all passed into the hands of Ilbert de Lacy, William the Conqueror's man in those parts, in recognition for his part in suppressing a revolt in 1070.

Shipley 1909 61865
In the foreground is a fine Victorian drinking fountain, and behind, the premises of Holdsworth the butcher. Most of the town's older properties are built from dark stone. A weekly market was held here. As there were no public houses in Saltaire, many of Titus Salt's workers ventured into the neighbouring town of Shipley, where they knew there were inns. However, if they over-indulged themselves and were brought up before the authorities they could expect no mercy - the teetotaller Titus Salt was one of Bradford's leading magistrates.

Shipley, The Glen 1909 61867
The beck tumbles down from the moor to join the River Aire at Shipley, its flow unimpeded by the profusion of huge boulders of millstone grit scattered throughout its bed. The textile workers of West Yorkshire were never very far from open moorland. All about there were high bilberry-covered slopes, rough grasses, broad skies full of larks, and bracing winds. Shipley Glen was one of the most popular beauty spots to which the people of Bradford flocked to escape the smoke and grime on their days off.

Shipley, The Glen 1909 61868
An amusement park was created at the summit in the late 1880s. The playground at Shipley Glen was originally in the ownership of a Colonel Maude, and he set about creating an amusement park for the masses. He built a boating pool and refreshment room, and installed swing boats and roundabouts. In 1900 the Glen and amusement park were purchased by Bradford Corporation. At weekends, they laid on extra services on the cable tramway which carried visitors keen to enjoy the spectacle to the top.

▼ **Shipley, The Glen 1921** 71640
Water is vital in wool processing, and the softer it is the better the finished product.
Despite its proximity to the Aire, and the apparent abundance of this fast-flowing
stream, Bradford was always short of water, which inspired mill owners to switch to
steampower. Many mills sank their own wells to ensure continuous supplies.

▼ **Greengates, Harrogate Road c1955** G115010
On the right is the local branch of the Co-op, a movement said to have
begun in Rochdale with just twenty-eight members and capital of just
£28. What would have been the retailer's profit after all his expenses
were handed back to the membership as a dividend?

▲ **Greengates, New Line c1955** G115009
Straight ahead at the
crossroads is New Line,
while to the left of
Glovers the tobacconist
and newsagent is the
Harrogate Road.

◄ Greengates, The Leeds and Liverpool Canal c1955 G115012

At 127 miles, this is the longest canal in Britain, and creates a vital trans-Pennine crossing between the mill towns of Yorkshire and the sea ports of the Mersey. It was designed to be a broad canal, with locks that could handle barges up to 14 feet wide. The scenery is magnificent; the canal threads a path through open moorland to the industrial backwaters of Shipley.

Greengates, Apperley Locks c1955 G115013

From Shipley the canal makes a long swing round a 500 ft-high hill to Apperley Bridge. Halfway round the curve, a set of three locks lowers the canal by 25 ft. Just beyond the Mitchell swing bridge, the Dobson Locks lower it a further 23 ft.

Hipperholme, High Street c1965 H211003

Hipperholme stands on an eminence, two miles from Halifax, and close to the Bradford and Halifax section of the L & Y Railway. It was a centre for the woollen manufactures, and for collieries, quarries and a tannery. The substantial-looking High Street buildings, reflect the village's prosperity.

Bingley, The Druids' Altar 1894 34759
This massive Millstone Grit boulder stands on a hillside strewn with rocks two miles outside Bingley on the Harden road. The land is part of the St Ives estate. Local antiquarians say that the cobbled way running from the Brown Cow inn towards the site is an old processional route walked by the Druids.

Bingley, From Ferncliff 1894 34744
A Victorian directory describes Bingley as standing 'on an eminence, amid wooded environs, with picturesque views, adjacent to the River Aire, the North Midland Railway, and the Leeds and Liverpool Canal'. It has ancient origins, and was named among the places given by William the Conqueror to his followers. There was an ancient castle here, long since disappeared. This broad prospect shows how the mills and manufactures gradually filled the landscape, turning a once modest village into a thriving town.

Bingley, The River Aire 1923 74415
The River Aire cuts a winding course through broad pastures, stony valleys and bustling industrial areas, on its way to join the Ouse and the open sea at Asselby Island. It joins the important Aire and Calder Navigation at Knottingley, where the waterway twists and turns for six miles. At Bingley, mills crowd down to the waterside.

Bingley, Five-Rise Locks 1894 34748
This magnificent flight of locks is on the Leeds and Liverpool Canal, and lifted barges a full sixty feet. Negotiating the flight was not for the faint-hearted - operating the paddles the wrong way could cause a tidal wave. The Leeds and Liverpool was designed to be a broad canal, with locks capable of handling barges up to 14 feet wide. Regular narrow boats had a width of just 7 feet.`

Bingley, The Old Market House 1894 34755

The Market House and Cross were built in 1753, and were originally sited in Main Street. In 1888 they were removed to the Prince of Wales Park. Here they were erected on the site of an old quarry. The Market House is constructed of five bays supported on rough-hewn square pillars. The stocks on the left were said to be the last in use in the county, and still in operation in the 1870s.

Bingley, Main Street 1926 79085

Bingley grew into a significant town, in Victorian times one long street of stone houses. In 1895 there was a town hall, two banks, a railway station, two substantial inns, a parish church, a free grammar school dating from 1529 and rebuilt in the late 19th century, and a public free library, opened in 1892. Its prosperity was founded on worsted yarn, dress goods, ironfounding, tanning and malting.

Bingley, Main Street 1926 79084
This gently curving tree-lined street is paved with stone setts. On the right the awnings are down so it must be a sunny day. A boy is selling milk in churns from a small pony-drawn cart. Bingley had a weekly market, formerly held on Tuesdays, and cattle fairs held on the first Tuesday in April and the second Tuesday in October.

Bingley, Main Street c1955 B98012
This view shows Main Street thirty years later than in the previous view. Some of the trees have gone and the old setts have been taken up and the surface tarmacked. Trolleybuses have replaced the trams. On the left is the Midland Hotel.

Index

Frith Book Co Titles

www.francisfrith.co.uk

The Frith Book Company publishes over 100 new titles each year. A selection of those currently available is listed below. For latest catalogue please contact Frith Book Co.
Town Books 96 pages, approximately 100 photos. **County and Themed Books** 128 pages, approximately 150 photos (unless specified). All titles hardback with laminated case and jacket, except those indicated pb (paperback)

Amersham, Chesham & Rickmansworth (pb)	1-85937-340-2	£9.99	Devon (pb)	1-85937-297-x	£9.99
Andover (pb)	1-85937-292-9	£9.99	Devon Churches (pb)	1-85937-250-3	£9.99
Aylesbury (pb)	1-85937-227-9	£9.99	Dorchester (pb)	1-85937-307-0	£9.99
Barnstaple (pb)	1-85937-300-3	£9.99	Dorset (pb)	1-85937-269-4	£9.99
Basildon Living Memories (pb)	1-85937-515-4	£9.99	Dorset Coast (pb)	1-85937-299-6	£9.99
Bath (pb)	1-85937-419-0	£9.99	Dorset Living Memories (pb)	1-85937-584-7	£9.99
Bedford (pb)	1-85937-205-8	£9.99	Down the Severn (pb)	1-85937-560-x	£9.99
Bedfordshire Living Memories	1-85937-513-8	£14.99	Down The Thames (pb)	1-85937-278-3	£9.99
Belfast (pb)	1-85937-303-8	£9.99	Down the Trent	1-85937-311-9	£14.99
Berkshire (pb)	1-85937-191-4	£9.99	East Anglia (pb)	1-85937-265-1	£9.99
Berkshire Churches	1-85937-170-1	£17.99	East Grinstead (pb)	1-85937-138-8	£9.99
Berkshire Living Memories	1-85937-332-1	£14.99	East London	1-85937-080-2	£14.99
Black Country	1-85937-497-2	£12.99	East Sussex (pb)	1-85937-606-1	£9.99
Blackpool (pb)	1-85937-393-3	£9.99	Eastbourne (pb)	1-85937-399-2	£9.99
Bognor Regis (pb)	1-85937-431-x	£9.99	Edinburgh (pb)	1-85937-193-0	£8.99
Bournemouth (pb)	1-85937-545-6	£9.99	England In The 1880s	1-85937-331-3	£17.99
Bradford (pb)	1-85937-204-x	£9.99	Essex - Second Selection	1-85937-456-5	£14.99
Bridgend (pb)	1-85937-386-0	£7.99	Essex (pb)	1-85937-270-8	£9.99
Bridgwater (pb)	1-85937-305-4	£9.99	Essex Coast	1-85937-342-9	£14.99
Bridport (pb)	1-85937-327-5	£9.99	Essex Living Memories	1-85937-490-5	£14.99
Brighton (pb)	1-85937-192-2	£8.99	Exeter	1-85937-539-1	£9.99
Bristol (pb)	1-85937-264-3	£9.99	Exmoor (pb)	1-85937-608-8	£9.99
British Life A Century Ago (pb)	1-85937-213-9	£9.99	Falmouth (pb)	1-85937-594-4	£9.99
Buckinghamshire (pb)	1-85937-200-7	£9.99	Folkestone (pb)	1-85937-124-8	£9.99
Camberley (pb)	1-85937-222-8	£9.99	Frome (pb)	1-85937-317-8	£9.99
Cambridge (pb)	1-85937-422-0	£9.99	Glamorgan	1-85937-488-3	£14.99
Cambridgeshire (pb)	1-85937-420-4	£9.99	Glasgow (pb)	1-85937-190-6	£9.99
Cambridgeshire Villages	1-85937-523-5	£14.99	Glastonbury (pb)	1-85937-338-0	£7.99
Canals And Waterways (pb)	1-85937-291-0	£9.99	Gloucester (pb)	1-85937-232-5	£9.99
Canterbury Cathedral (pb)	1-85937-179-5	£9.99	Gloucestershire (pb)	1-85937-561-8	£9.99
Cardiff (pb)	1-85937-093-4	£9.99	Great Yarmouth (pb)	1-85937-426-3	£9.99
Carmarthenshire (pb)	1-85937-604-5	£9.99	Greater Manchester (pb)	1-85937-266-x	£9.99
Chelmsford (pb)	1-85937-310-0	£9.99	Guildford (pb)	1-85937-410-7	£9.99
Cheltenham (pb)	1-85937-095-0	£9.99	Hampshire (pb)	1-85937-279-1	£9.99
Cheshire (pb)	1-85937-271-6	£9.99	Harrogate (pb)	1-85937-423-9	£9.99
Chester (pb)	1-85937-382 8	£9.99	Hastings and Bexhill (pb)	1-85937-131-0	£9.99
Chesterfield (pb)	1-85937-378-x	£9.99	Heart of Lancashire (pb)	1-85937-197-3	£9.99
Chichester (pb)	1-85937-228-7	£9.99	Helston (pb)	1-85937-214-7	£9.99
Churches of East Cornwall (pb)	1-85937-249-x	£9.99	Hereford (pb)	1-85937-175-2	£9.99
Churches of Hampshire (pb)	1-85937-207-4	£9.99	Herefordshire (pb)	1-85937-567-7	£9.99
Cinque Ports & Two Ancient Towns	1-85937-492-1	£14.99	Herefordshire Living Memories	1-85937-514-6	£14.99
Colchester (pb)	1-85937-188-4	£8.99	Hertfordshire (pb)	1-85937-247-3	£9.99
Cornwall (pb)	1-85937-229-5	£9.99	Horsham (pb)	1-85937-432-8	£9.99
Cornwall Living Memories	1-85937-248-1	£14.99	Humberside (pb)	1-85937-605-3	£9.99
Cotswolds (pb)	1-85937-230-9	£9.99	Hythe, Romney Marsh, Ashford (pb)	1-85937-256-2	£9.99
Cotswolds Living Memories	1-85937-255-4	£14.99	Ipswich (pb)	1-85937-424-7	£9.99
County Durham (pb)	1-85937-398-4	£9.99	Isle of Man (pb)	1-85937-268-6	£9.99
Croydon Living Memories (pb)	1-85937-162-0	£9.99	Isle of Wight (pb)	1-85937-429-8	£9.99
Cumbria (pb)	1-85937-621-5	£9.99	Isle of Wight Living Memories	1-85937-304-6	£14.99
Derby (pb)	1-85937-367-4	£9.99	Kent (pb)	1-85937-189-2	£9.99
Derbyshire (pb)	1-85937-196-5	£9.99	Kent Living Memories(pb)	1-85937-401-8	£9.99
Derbyshire Living Memories	1-85937-330-5	£14.99	Kings Lynn (pb)	1-85937-334-8	£9.99

Available from your local bookshop or from the publisher

Frith Book Co Titles (continued)

Lake District (pb)	1-85937-275-9	£9.99	Sherborne (pb)	1-85937-301-1	£9.99
Lancashire Living Memories	1-85937-335-6	£14.99	Shrewsbury (pb)	1-85937-325-9	£9.99
Lancaster, Morecambe, Heysham (pb)	1-85937-233-3	£9.99	Shropshire (pb)	1-85937-326-7	£9.99
Leeds (pb)	1-85937-202-3	£9.99	Shropshire Living Memories	1-85937-643-6	£14.99
Leicester (pb)	1-85937-381-x	£9.99	Somerset	1-85937-153-1	£14.99
Leicestershire & Rutland Living Memories	1-85937-500-6	£12.99	South Devon Coast	1-85937-107-8	£14.99
Leicestershire (pb)	1-85937-185-x	£9.99	South Devon Living Memories (pb)	1-85937-609-6	£9.99
Lighthouses	1-85937-257-0	£9.99	South East London (pb)	1-85937-263-5	£9.99
Lincoln (pb)	1-85937-380-1	£9.99	South Somerset	1-85937-318-6	£14.99
Lincolnshire (pb)	1-85937-433-6	£9.99	South Wales	1-85937-519-7	£14.99
Liverpool and Merseyside (pb)	1-85937-234-1	£9.99	Southampton (pb)	1-85937-427-1	£9.99
London (pb)	1-85937-183-3	£9.99	Southend (pb)	1-85937-313-5	£9.99
London Living Memories	1-85937-454-9	£14.99	Southport (pb)	1-85937-425-5	£9.99
Ludlow (pb)	1-85937-176-0	£9.99	St Albans (pb)	1-85937-341-0	£9.99
Luton (pb)	1-85937-235-x	£9.99	St Ives (pb)	1-85937-415-8	£9.99
Maidenhead (pb)	1-85937-339-9	£9.99	Stafford Living Memories (pb)	1-85937-503-0	£9.99
Maidstone (pb)	1-85937-391-7	£9.99	Staffordshire (pb)	1-85937-308-9	£9.99
Manchester (pb)	1-85937-198-1	£9.99	Stourbridge (pb)	1-85937-530-8	£9.99
Marlborough (pb)	1-85937-336-4	£9.99	Stratford upon Avon (pb)	1-85937-388-7	£9.99
Middlesex	1-85937-158-2	£14.99	Suffolk (pb)	1-85937-221-x	£9.99
Monmouthshire	1-85937-532-4	£14.99	Suffolk Coast (pb)	1-85937-610-x	£9.99
New Forest (pb)	1-85937-390-9	£9.99	Surrey (pb)	1-85937-240-6	£9.99
Newark (pb)	1-85937-366-6	£9.99	Surrey Living Memories	1-85937-328-3	£14.99
Newport, Wales (pb)	1-85937-258-9	£9.99	Sussex (pb)	1-85937-184-1	£9.99
Newquay (pb)	1-85937-421-2	£9.99	Sutton (pb)	1-85937-337-2	£9.99
Norfolk (pb)	1-85937-195-7	£9.99	Swansea (pb)	1-85937-167-1	£9.99
Norfolk Broads	1-85937-486-7	£14.99	Taunton (pb)	1-85937-314-3	£9.99
Norfolk Living Memories (pb)	1-85937-402-6	£9.99	Tees Valley & Cleveland (pb)	1-85937-623-1	£9.99
North Buckinghamshire	1-85937-626-6	£14.99	Teignmouth (pb)	1-85937-370-4	£7.99
North Devon Living Memories	1-85937-261-9	£14.99	Thanet (pb)	1-85937-116-7	£9.99
North Hertfordshire	1-85937-547-2	£14.99	Tiverton (pb)	1-85937-178-7	£9.99
North London (pb)	1-85937-403-4	£9.99	Torbay (pb)	1-85937-597-9	£9.99
North Somerset	1-85937-302-x	£14.99	Truro (pb)	1-85937-598-7	£9.99
North Wales (pb)	1-85937-298-8	£9.99	Victorian & Edwardian Dorset	1-85937-254-6	£14.99
North Yorkshire (pb)	1-85937-236-8	£9.99	Victorian & Edwardian Kent (pb)	1-85937-624-X	£9.99
Northamptonshire Living Memories	1-85937-529-4	£14.99	Victorian & Edwardian Maritime Album (pb)	1-85937-622-3	£9.99
Northamptonshire	1-85937-150-7	£14.99	Victorian and Edwardian Sussex (pb)	1-85937-625-8	£9.99
Northumberland Tyne & Wear (pb)	1-85937-281-3	£9.99	Villages of Devon (pb)	1-85937-293-7	£9.99
Northumberland	1-85937-522-7	£14.99	Villages of Kent (pb)	1-85937-294-5	£9.99
Norwich (pb)	1-85937-194-9	£8.99	Villages of Sussex (pb)	1-85937-295-3	£9.99
Nottingham (pb)	1-85937-324-0	£9.99	Warrington (pb)	1-85937-507-3	£9.99
Nottinghamshire (pb)	1-85937-187-6	£9.99	Warwick (pb)	1-85937-518-9	£9.99
Oxford (pb)	1-85937-411-5	£9.99	Warwickshire (pb)	1-85937-203-1	£9.99
Oxfordshire (pb)	1-85937-430-1	£9.99	Welsh Castles (pb)	1-85937-322-4	£9.99
Oxfordshire Living Memories	1-85937-525-1	£14.99	West Midlands (pb)	1-85937-289-9	£9.99
Paignton (pb)	1-85937-374-7	£7.99	West Sussex (pb)	1-85937-607-x	£9.99
Peak District (pb)	1-85937-280-5	£9.99	West Yorkshire (pb)	1-85937-201-5	£9.99
Pembrokeshire	1-85937-262-7	£14.99	Weston Super Mare (pb)	1-85937-306-2	£9.99
Penzance (pb)	1-85937-595-2	£9.99	Weymouth (pb)	1-85937-209-0	£9.99
Peterborough (pb)	1-85937-219-8	£9.99	Wiltshire (pb)	1-85937-277-5	£9.99
Picturesque Harbours	1-85937-208-2	£14.99	Wiltshire Churches (pb)	1-85937-171-x	£9.99
Piers	1-85937-237-6	£17.99	Wiltshire Living Memories (pb)	1-85937-396-8	£9.99
Plymouth (pb)	1-85937-389-5	£9.99	Winchester (pb)	1-85937-428-x	£9.99
Poole & Sandbanks (pb)	1-85937-251-1	£9.99	Windsor (pb)	1-85937-333-x	£9.99
Preston (pb)	1-85937-212-0	£9.99	Wokingham & Bracknell (pb)	1-85937-329-1	£9.99
Reading (pb)	1-85937-238-4	£9.99	Woodbridge (pb)	1-85937-498-0	£9.99
Redhill to Reigate (pb)	1-85937-596-0	£9.99	Worcester (pb)	1-85937-165-5	£9.99
Ringwood (pb)	1-85937-384-4	£7.99	Worcestershire Living Memories	1-85937-489-1	£14.99
Romford (pb)	1-85937-319-4	£9.99	Worcestershire	1-85937-152-3	£14.99
Royal Tunbridge Wells (pb)	1-85937-504-9	£9.99	York (pb)	1-85937-199-x	£9.99
Salisbury (pb)	1-85937-239-2	£9.99	Yorkshire (pb)	1-85937-186-8	£9.99
Scarborough (pb)	1-85937-379-8	£9.99	Yorkshire Coastal Memories	1-85937-506-5	£14.99
Sevenoaks and Tonbridge (pb)	1-85937-392-5	£9.99	Yorkshire Dales	1-85937-502-2	£14.99
Sheffield & South Yorks (pb)	1-85937-267-8	£9.99	Yorkshire Living Memories (pb)	1-85937-397-6	£9.99

See Frith books on the internet at www.francisfrith.co.uk

FRITH PRODUCTS & SERVICES

Francis Frith would doubtless be pleased to know that the pioneering publishing venture he started in 1860 still continues today. Over a hundred and forty years later, The Francis Frith Collection continues in the same innovative tradition and is now one of the foremost publishers of vintage photographs in the world. Some of the current activities include:

Interior Decoration

Today Frith's photographs can be seen framed and as giant wall murals in thousands of pubs, restaurants, hotels, banks, retail stores and other public buildings throughout the country. In every case they enhance the unique local atmosphere of the places they depict and provide reminders of gentler days in an increasingly busy and frenetic world.

Product Promotions

Frith products are used by many major companies to promote the sales of their own products or to reinforce their own history and heritage. Frith promotions have been used by Hovis bread, Courage beers, Scots Porage Oats, Colman's mustard, Cadbury's foods, Mellow Birds coffee, Dunhill pipe tobacco, Guinness, and Bulmer's Cider.

Genealogy and Family History

As the interest in family history and roots grows world-wide, more and more people are turning to Frith's photographs of Great Britain for images of the towns, villages and streets where their ancestors lived; and, of course, photographs of the churches and chapels where their ancestors were christened, married and buried are an essential part of every genealogy tree and family album.

Frith Products

All Frith photographs are available Framed or just as Mounted Prints and Posters (size 23 x 16 inches). These may be ordered from the address below. From time to time other products - Address Books, Calendars, Table Mats, etc - are available.

The Internet

Already fifty thousand Frith photographs can be viewed and purchased on the internet through the Frith websites and a myriad of partner sites.

For more detailed information on Frith companies and products, look at these sites:

www.francisfrith.co.uk
www.francisfrith.com
(for North American visitors)

See the complete list of Frith Books at:

www.francisfrith.co.uk

This web site is regularly updated with the latest list of publications from the Frith Book Company. If you wish to buy books relating to another part of the country that your local bookshop does not stock, you may purchase on-line.

For further information, trade, or author enquiries please contact us at the address below:
The Francis Frith Collection, Frith's Barn, Teffont, Salisbury, Wiltshire, England SP3 5QP.
Tel: +44 (0)1722 716 376 Fax: +44 (0)1722 716 881   Email: sales@francisfrith.co.uk

See Frith books on the internet at www.francisfrith.co.uk

FREE MOUNTED PRINT

Mounted Print
Overall size 14 x 11 inches

Fill in and cut out this voucher and return
it with your remittance for £2.25 (to cover postage and handling). Offer valid for delivery to UK addresses only.

Choose any photograph included in this book.
Your SEPIA print will be A4 in size. It will be mounted in a cream mount with a burgundy rule line (overall size 14 x 11 inches).

**Order additional Mounted Prints
at HALF PRICE (only £7.49 each*)**
If you would like to order more Frith prints from this book, possibly as gifts for friends and family, you can buy them at half price (with no additional postage and handling costs).

Have your Mounted Prints framed
For an extra £14.95 per print* you can have your mounted print(s) framed in an elegant polished wood and gilt moulding, overall size 16 x 13 inches (no additional postage and handling required).

---

* IMPORTANT!

These special prices are only available if you order at the same time as you order your free mounted print. You must use the ORIGINAL VOUCHER on this page (no copies permitted). We can only despatch to one address.

Send completed Voucher form to:
The Francis Frith Collection, Frith's Barn, Teffont, Salisbury, Wiltshire SP3 5QP

Please do not photocopy this voucher. Only the original is valid, so please fill it in, cut it out and return it to us with your order.

Picture ref no	Page no	Qty	Mounted @ £7.49	Framed + £14.95	Total Cost
		1	Free of charge*	£	£
			£7.49	£	£
			£7.49	£	£
			£7.49	£	£
			£7.49	£	£
			£7.49	£	£

Please allow 28 days for delivery

* Post & handling (UK)	£2.25
Total Order Cost	£

Title of this book . . . .

I enclose a cheque/postal order for £ . . . .

made payable to 'The Francis Frith Collection'

OR please debit my Mastercard / Visa / Switch / Amex card
(credit cards please on all overseas orders), details below

Card Number

Issue No (Switch only)   Valid from (Amex/Switch)

Expires   Signature

Name Mr/Mrs/Ms . . . .

Address . . . .

. . . .

. . . .

. . . . Postcode . . . .

Daytime Tel No . . . .

Email . . . .

Valid to 31/12/05

Would you like to find out more about Francis Frith?

We have recently recruited some entertaining speakers who are happy to visit local groups, clubs and societies to give an illustrated talk documenting Frith's travels and photographs. If you are a member of such a group and are interested in hosting a presentation, we would love to hear from you.

Our speakers bring with them a small selection of our local town and county books, together with sample prints. They are happy to take orders. A small proportion of the order value is donated to the group who have hosted the presentation. The talks are therefore an excellent way of fundraising for small groups and societies.

Can you help us with information about any of the Frith photographs in this book?

We are gradually compiling an historical record for each of the photographs in the Frith archive. It is always fascinating to find out the names of the people shown in the pictures, as well as insights into the shops, buildings and other features depicted.

If you recognize anyone in the photographs in this book, or if you have information not already included in the author's caption, do let us know. We would love to hear from you, and will try to publish it in future books or articles.

Our production team

Frith books are produced by a small dedicated team at offices in the converted Grade II listed 18th-century barn at Teffont near Salisbury, illustrated above. Most have worked with the Frith Collection for many years. All have in common one quality: they have a passion for the Frith Collection. The team is constantly expanding, but currently includes:

Paul Baron, Jason Buck, John Buck, Ruth Butler, Heather Crisp, David Davies, Isobel Hall, Julian Hight, Peter Horne, James Kinnear, Karen Kinnear, Tina Leary, Stuart Login, David Marsh, Sue Molloy, Glenda Morgan, Wayne Morgan, Kate Rotondetto, Dean Scource, Eliza Sackett, Terence Sackett, Sandra Sampson, Adrian Sanders, Sandra Sanger, Julia Skinner, Claire Tarrier, Lewis Taylor, Shelley Tolcher, Lorraine Tuck and Jeremy Walker.